TRAVEL WITH THE GREAT EXPLORERS

Explore with
Francisco Vázquez de Coronado

WITHDRAWN

Tim Cooke

Crabtree Publishing Company
www.crabtreebooks.com

Crabtree Publishing Company
www.crabtreebooks.com

Author: Tim Cooke

Designer: Lynne Lennon

Picture Manager: Sophie Mortimer

Design Manager: Keith Davis

Editorial Director: Lindsey Lowe

Children's Publisher: Anne O'Daly

Crabtree Editorial Director: Kathy Middleton

Crabtree Editor: Petrice Custance

Proofreader: Wendy Scavuzzo

**Production coordinator
   and prepress technician:** Tammy McGarr

Print coordinator: Katherine Berti

Photographs:

Front Cover: Dreamstime: Rinus Baak tr; **NPS Photo:** Coronado National Memorial l; **Shutterstock:** Sumiko Photo cr, Macro Wildlife br.

Interior: Alamy: Art Archive 24, Glasshouse Images 10, National Geographic Creative 18-19t, North Wind Picture Archives 29, Prisma Archivo 28tr, Prisma Bildagentur AG 28bl, The Protected Art Archive 21; **Alfa Image:** Public Domain 5br; **Scott Catron:** marco1952 19tr; **Denver Public Library:** Western History Department: 18b; **Dreamstime:** 23t, Rinus Baak 15br, Brian Creed 27c, Bambi L. Dingman 7, Joan Egert 23b, Zacarias Pereira Da Mata 13b, Krzysztof Slusarczyk 25br, Ryszard Stelmachowicz 17t; **Library of Congress:** 11, 14-15b, 20, 20-21b, 27t; **NARA:** 26; **NPS Photo:** Coronado National Memorial 4; **PHGCOM:** Musée de l'Armée 15t; **Rijksmuseum:** 6r; **Shutterstock:** 13t, 17b, Amy K Casillas 16, Anton Foltin 22, Jang Hongyan 17c, Eric Isselélee 13, Josemaria Toscano 6bl, Luis Carlos Torres 10br; **Stanford University:** 5t; **Thinkstock:** 24-25c; **Topfoto:** The Granger Collection 12; **WCC:** History of England 14l.

Written and produced for Crabtree Publishing Company by Brown Bear Books

Brown Bear Books has made every attempt to contact the copyright holder. If you have any information please contact licensing@brownbearbooks.co.uk

Library and Archives Canada Cataloguing in Publication

Cooke, Tim, 1961-, author
      Explore with Francisco Vazquez de Coronado / Tim Cooke.

(Travel with the great explorers)
Includes index.
Issued in print and electronic formats.
ISBN 978-0-7787-2847-4 (hardback).--ISBN 978-0-7787-2851-1 (paperback).--ISBN 978-1-4271-7726-1 (html)

      1. Coronado, Francisco Vásquez de, 1510-1554--Juvenile literature. 2. Explorers--America--Biography--Juvenile literature. 3. Explorers--Spain--Biography--Juvenile literature. 4. Southwest, New--Description and travel--Juvenile literature. 5. America--Discovery and exploration--Spanish--Juvenile literature.
I. Title. II. Series: Travel with the great explorers

E125.V3C64 2016   j910'.92   C2016-903341-4
                                                         C2016-903342-2

Library of Congress Cataloging-in-Publication Data

Names: Cooke, Tim, 1961- author.
Title: Explore with Francisco Vazquez de Coronado / Tim Cooke.
Description: New York : Crabtree Publishing Company, [2016] | Series: Travel with the great explorers | Includes index.
Identifiers: LCCN 2016023648 (print) | LCCN 2016024182 (ebook) | ISBN 9780778728474 (reinforced library binding) | ISBN 9780778728511 (pbk.) | ISBN 9781427177261 (electronic HTML)
Subjects: LCSH: Coronado, Francisco Vásquez de, 1510-1554--Juvenile literature. | Explorers--America--Biography--Juvenile literature. | Explorers--Spain--Biography--Juvenile literature. | Southwest, New--Description and travel--Juvenile literature. | America--Discovery and exploration--Spanish--Juvenile literature.
Classification: LCC E125.V3 C64 2016 (print) | LCC E125.V3 (ebook) | DDC 910.92 [B] --dc23
LC record available at https://lccn.loc.gov/2016023648

Crabtree Publishing Company
www.crabtreebooks.com   1-800-387-7650

Printed in Canada/072016/EF20160630

Published in Canada
Crabtree Publishing
616 Welland Ave.
St. Catharines, ON
L2M 5V6

Published in the United States
Crabtree Publishing
PMB 59051
350 Fifth Avenue, 59th Floor
New York, New York 10118

Published in the United Kingdom
Crabtree Publishing
Maritime House
Basin Road North, Hove
BN41 1WR

Published in Australia
Crabtree Publishing
3 Charles Street
Coburg North
VIC, 3058

CONTENTS

Meet the Boss

Francisco Vázquez de Coronado left Spain as a young man to seek his fortune in the Americas. He would lead an important expedition into what is now the Southwestern United States.

Did you know?

In New Spain, Coronado heard stories about gold. Spanish explorer Álvar Núñez Cabeza de Vaca had led an unsuccessful expedition to find Cibola—a region said to contain the Seven Cities of Gold.

LIMITED OPPORTUNITIES

+ Younger sons inherit nothing

Francisco Vázquez de Coronado (also Vásquez) was born in 1510, the second son of a wealthy family in Salamanca, Spain. His older brother **inherited** the family's wealth, so Coronado had to make his own fortune. Like many young Spaniards of the time, Coronado decided to seek his fortune in the **empire** Spain was creating in the "New World," meaning the Americas. In 1535, he traveled to New Spain (present-day Mexico) with his friend, Antonio de Mendoza. Mendoza was the first **viceroy** of New Spain.

A HELPFUL MARRIAGE

★ Happy and profitable union

In Mexico City, Coronado worked for Mendoza in the Spanish government. He also married Beatriz de Estrada, the daughter of a senior Spanish official. Beatriz was only 12, while Coronado was about 27. Such marriages would not be allowed today, but were sometimes made at that time for social or political reasons. Through Beatriz, Coronado acquired one of the largest **estates** in New Spain. The couple later had eight children.

Enslaved

The Spaniards had conquered Mexico in 1521. Many of the Native peoples living there, such as the Aztec, had died from diseases brought by the Spaniards. The rest had been enslaved.

New Galicia

My Explorer Journal

★ Imagine that you are just like Coronado, and your chances of earning a decent living at home are limited. Write a letter to your parents explaining your reasons for wanting to sail to New Spain.

GAINING PROMOTION

+ Shows loyalty to the Spanish crown

Coronado worked hard for Viceroy Mendoza. The Spaniards forced Native slaves to work in gold and silver mines. The slaves rebelled to try to gain their freedom. Coronado helped end the rebellions by force. Mendoza rewarded Coronado by making him governor of the frontier **province** of New Galicia, shown on this old map (above left).

RUMORS FROM THE NORTH

☞ Hears of treasure

☞ Puts faith in a monk

Coronado wanted to discover new lands and gold for Spain. In 1539, he heard of a monk named Fray Marcos de Niza. The monk had traveled north of New Spain with a Moroccan slave named Estevan. Estevan had stayed with the Zuni people in Cibola. Fray Marcos returned to Mexico with stories of the wealthy city of Cibola. He claimed it was as large and rich as Mexico City itself. Coronado believed it must be one of the Seven Cities of Gold he had heard stories about.

Where Are We Heading?

Viceroy Mendoza and Coronado funded a large expedition to find Cibola. Coronado's journey covered more than 4,000 miles (6,437 km).

THE CITIES OF CIBOLA

☞ **Hard traveling through the desert...**

☞ **... leads to disappointment**

In July 1540, after traveling four months across deserts and over mountains, Coronado's expedition reached what they thought was the city of Cibola. But they did not find a city of gold. Instead, they found Hawikuh. Hawikuh was a **pueblo**, or a village of interlocking homes made from baked earth. The pueblo was home to the Zuni—a group of Native peoples also known as Pueblo peoples.

THE GRAND CANYON

+ **A first for Europeans**

Coronado and his men used the name "Cibola," not only for the city they hoped to find, but also for the whole region. Coronado sent out groups to explore this region. García López de Cárdenas and his team used guides from the local Hopi people to march north. After 20 days, he and his men reached the edge of a huge gorge with a river far below, making them the first Europeans to see the Grand Canyon.

PAINTED DESERT

+ Beautiful... but inhospitable

One group of Spaniards traveled northeast of Cibola, exploring what is now known as the Colorado **Plateau**. They also came across the Painted Desert (below), where layers of rock create a multicolored display. Also called **badlands**, the area covers 7,500 square miles (19,425 sq km).

> **The country itself is the best I have ever seen for producing all the products of Spain...what I am sure of is that there is not any gold nor any other metal in all that country."** *Francisco de Coronado, writing about Quivira.*

RENEWED HOPE

★ **Coronado believes the "Turk"**

★ **Crosses the grasslands**

In spring 1541, Coronado headed north from the region he called Cibola. A Pawnee prisoner known as the "Turk" had told him stories about a magnificent city called Quivira. Coronado thought this must be one of the Cities of Gold. The Spaniards crossed the plains of what is now the Texas Panhandle to Kansas. When they reached Quivira, they found a farming settlement of grass-covered huts.

CORONADO'S JOURNEY THROUGH THE SOUTHWEST

Coronado traveled more than 4,000 miles (6,440 km) in a little more than two years. His journey took him through what is now known as New Mexico, Arizona, Texas, and Kansas, crossing open deserts and vast seas of grass.

NORTH AMERICA

Quivira

Grand Canyon

Taos
Pecos

Tiguex

Hawikuh

Acoma

Rio Grande

NEW SPAIN

Culiacán

Compostella

NEW GALICIA

Grand Canyon
A group of Spaniards led by García López de Cárdenas became the first Europeans to see the Grand Canyon in September 1540. Coronado had sent them north to seek a great river he had heard stories about.

Hawikuh
When Coronado arrived at what he hoped was Cibola, he did not find a city of gold but a mud-built village of the Zuni people named Hawikuh. The Spaniards called the village and its surrounding region Cibola.

Tiguex
In the cold winter of 1540, the Spaniards demanded that the Tiwa of Tiguex pueblo give them blankets. When the Tiwa hesitated, the Spaniards attacked, killing many people inside the village.

Culiacán
Culiacán was the last Spanish settlement the expedition passed before it left New Spain. Spaniards who had overpacked their horses gave away many of their possessions there.

Quivira

Coronado hoped to find another "City of Gold" at Quivira, in what is now Kansas. Instead, he found a farming village of the Wichita people. The explorer had to accept that he was not going to find gold.

Locator map

Key

- - - - ► **Main expedition**

........► **Secondary expeditions**

Scale $\dfrac{200 \text{ miles}}{320 \text{ km}}$

Great Plains

Coronado and the Spaniards had never seen anything like the vast grasslands of Texas and Kansas—or the millions of buffalo that lived there. They had to use a compass to find their way through the featureless landscape.

Palo Duro

In late spring 1541, the expedition rested in the steep-sided Palo Duro Canyon (in present-day Texas). There they met **nomadic** Apache bands who survived by hunting buffalo on the plains.

Meet the Crew

The huge expedition Coronado led from Mexico included some of the leading nobles of New Spain, together with thousands of Native servants and slaves.

Bigotes

A key member of Coronado's expedition was a Pecos chief who guided them to the Great Plains. He had a large moustache, so the Spaniards called him Bigotes, Spanish for "whiskers."

THE EXPEDITION

+ Thousands of people...

+ ... and twice as many animals

Coronado led up to 400 Europeans, including many Spanish nobles eager to make their fortunes. There were also four monks who wanted to **convert** Native peoples to Christianity. The monks included Fray Marcos de Niza, who acted as a guide. The expedition also included nearly 2,000 Native people, including women and children, and a number of black servants. The expedition took herds of pigs, sheep, and cattle to provide food.

TALL TALES

★ **Would a priest lie?**

★ **Or was it a mistake?**

The Spaniards were desperate to find new sources of gold and silver. They eagerly listened to the story Fray Marcos told about Cibola. When Fray Marcos led the expedition to Hawikuh in July 1540, Coronado was disappointed to find only a pueblo village. Marcos explained that he had only seen Cibola from a distance. Coronado called him a liar and sent him back to Mexico City.

My Explorer Journal

★ **Imagine that you are Coronado. Write an advertisement to try to recruit men to join your expedition. List the qualities you think they will need.**

Pedro de Castañeda is the main reason we know so much about Coronado's expedition. He accompanied Coronado and wrote an account of the trip that includes detailed descriptions of the different Native peoples the Spaniards met. Castañeda described the landscapes the expedition crossed and why Coronado eventually gave up. However, Castañeda wrote his account 20 years after the expedition had taken place, so his memories might not have been reliable.

HERNANDO DE ALARCÓN

+ Waits two months... in vain

Viceroy Antonio de Mendoza sent the **navigator** Hernando de Alarcón to sail up the coast from New Spain with supplies for Coronado's expedition. Alarcón set sail on May 9, 1540, but was unable to meet with Coronado. He did manage to reach the Colorado River, which he named Buena Guia, and became the first European to sail up its lower part. Unlike other Spaniards, when Alarcón met Native peoples he was said to have treated them well, and never used violence.

THE TURK

★ Coronado led astray

The "Turk" was the name the Spaniards gave to a Pawnee tribesman being held prisoner by the Pueblo peoples. His clothes reminded them of those worn by Turkish people. The Turk offered to lead the Spaniards to a city named Quivira. He probably hoped to **lure** them away from the pueblos to protect his own people.

Check Out the Ride

Leading a large expedition into unfamiliar territory was very challenging. The wealthier Spaniards relied on horses for transportation—everyone else walked alongside them.

HORSES

+ New animals in America

+ Horsemen inexperienced

There were approximately 1,200 horses on the expedition. Each **cavalryman** had at least one horse. Coronado himself took as many as 23 horses. The animals allowed the men to cover great distances. The Spaniards had introduced horses to North America in 1519, which was the first time Native peoples had seen horses. It was a long time before Native peoples began to use horses.

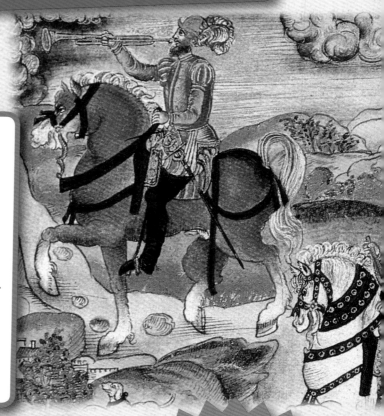

TRAVEL UPDATE

Get packing!

★ If you're joining an expedition, you better learn how to pack a horse! Some Spaniards took so many possessions they could not load them all on their horses. They had to give many of their belongings away before they left New Spain. In addition, some of the horses were lazy and out of shape. In the first month, the expedition only traveled 350 miles (563 km).

Slow Moving

Historians have worked out that the Coronado expedition covered around 12 miles (19 km) a day. They were slowed down by the large herd of animals that traveled along with them.

ALL KINDS OF ANIMALS

★ **Food on the hoof**

★ **Animals slow the expedition down**

The horses were the kings of the animals on the expedition, but there were many other animals. Mules carried equipment, and fierce dogs were used for hunting or to scare Native peoples. To guarantee a supply of food, there were herds of cattle, sheep, goats, and hogs. They moved slowly—and needed lots of grass!

Did you know?

Each day, a group of horsemen rode ahead of the expedition. They would find a place to camp and look for food. Then they waited for the others to catch up.

ON THE WATER

☞ **Sailing up the coast...**

☞ **... and into a river**

Governor Mendoza ordered Hernando de Alarcón to sail up the coast of New Spain into the Gulf of California. At sea, Alarcón used sturdy sailing ships named **caravels** (left). When he reached the Colorado River, however, the caravels could not sail against the strong current. Instead, Alarcón explored the river in two large rowing boats, each powered by 20 rowers.

Solve It With Science

The Spaniards used European inventions on their expedition. Meanwhile, the Native peoples they met had also developed their own technologies.

Plain Travel

The Teyas of the plains navigated by firing an arrow in the direction they wanted to travel. They walked to the arrow, then fired another, and so on. This meant they always walked in the right direction.

TRAVEL UPDATE

All at sea in the grass

Navigators! You might be used to using a magnetic **compass** (left) to find directions at sea—but remember to bring it if you're crossing the Great Plains. Coronado's men found the grass was so tall the back of the expedition couldn't see the front. There were no hills, trees, or rock formations to act as landmarks. Coronado had to use a compass to navigate. The forward party left piles of buffalo bones to mark the path.

A NEW RIVER

★ **Alarcón finds the Colorado**

★ **Proves Baja California is peninsula**

Hernando de Alarcón spent three months sailing up the west coast but eventually found his way blocked. This proved that California was not an island, as earlier explorers thought (right). Baja California was a **peninsula**. At the top of the Gulf of California, Alarcón crossed **sandbars** to enter the Colorado River.

GUNPOWDER!

☛ Spaniards have cannons and guns

☛ Enemies have stones and arrows

The Spaniards had guns and six bronze cannons. They thought gunpowder weapons would give them an advantage over Native peoples, but they were wrong. The cannon balls were not powerful enough to knock down the strong walls of Native pueblos, and the Spaniards ran low on gunpowder. In addition, the bows and arrows of their enemies proved highly effective.

STURDY BUILDINGS

+ Homes built from adobe

+ Located on top of cliffs

Did you know?

Instead of using stones for building, the Tiwa people of the Tiguex region mixed coals, ashes, dirt, and water to make balls of clay that they piled together to make walls.

Pueblos were designed to be easy to defend. The separate dwellings were built together in a single block with no front entrance. The only way in was from the roof, which was reached by ladders that could be pulled up. In addition, some pueblos stood on top of rocky cliffs, or **mesas**. The pueblo walls were made from **adobe**. Adobe was made by mixing ashes, earth, and coals made from burned twigs.

Hanging at Home

The Spaniards did not know what to expect in North America. They took the wrong clothing and not enough food. For much of the time, they were cold and hungry.

Did you know?

While stopped in the Spanish town of Culiacan, Coronado and his men gave away many clothes, as they had packed too much. When winter came, however, they regretted their generosity!

WATCH THE WEATHER!

- Spaniards not properly prepared
- Bitter winter takes its toll

Coronado and his party came from Spain and Mexico, so most of them were used to warm weather. During the winter of 1540, snow fell continually for two months, covering the landscape and wiping out trails. Every night, the men had to clear away snow to make their camp. In the summer, on the other hand, the Southwest was hot and dry. Finding fresh water was a constant problem.

WE WANT TO STAY HERE!

★ Spaniards live in pueblos

The Spanish expedition moved slowly, even with their horses. It took five months to reach Hawikuh. The Spaniards forced the local Zuni peoples to hand over food and allow them to stay in Zuni villages for six weeks. The same pattern occurred as the Spaniards moved on to other pueblos. They asked the Native peoples for accommodation and food—and took them if they were not freely given.

WE ARE FREEZING!

The explorers' clothing was not warm enough for snow and hail. Coronado asked the Tiwa people of the Tiguex pueblos for blankets and clothing for his freezing men. The Spaniards had already seized food from the villages, however, so the Tiwa resisted these new demands.

My Explorer Journal

★ The Spaniards described a storm when hailstones broke crockery, dented their helmets, destroyed their tents, and injured their horses. Write an imaginative account of being stuck in such a violent hailstorm.

FAMISHED!

★ **Explorers run short of food**

Coronado thought he had enough food when the expedition began. After he failed to meet up with Alarcón and his supply ships, however, getting enough to eat became difficult. Coronado wrote to New Spain to ask for more supplies. Meanwhile, his men relied on the generosity of the local peoples. They grew corn, and Pedro de Castañeda later recalled that Coronado thought the corncakes they made were the best thing he had ever tasted.

TRAVEL UPDATE

This is for you

★ If you're visiting the pueblos, take plenty of gifts. **Etiquette** requires an exchange of presents between hosts and visitors. The Spaniards gave the Pueblo peoples glass beads and copper bells. In return, the Spaniards received **turquoise**, cloth, skins, turkeys, and buffalo meat. The people of Cicuye gave them a prisoner from another tribe. The Spaniards nicknamed him the "Turk."

Meeting and Greeting

Coronado's search for the Cities of Gold took him to the adobe villages in what is now New Mexico and Arizona. Some of the peoples welcomed the Spaniards—others were more wary.

FIRST CONTACT

- Tempers flare in Cibola
- Coronado nearly killed

In July 1540, the expedition reached what they expected to be Cibola. In fact, it was the village of Hawikuh, home of the Zuni peoples. Coronado demanded food for his men, who were starving. The Zuni found the strangers rude, and refused. The Spaniards attacked the pueblo with cannons and guns, and the Zuni defended themselves with arrows and stones. In one attack, Coronado had to be rescued. The Spaniards broke into the pueblo (right). They seized food— but they also realized that Cibola was not a City of Gold.

IN THE PUEBLOS

★ Native peoples reject Spaniards...

★ ... or cooperate to avoid trouble

Coronado divided his expedition at Hawikuh so his men could search a larger area for the Cities of Gold (left). Instead, they found only more pueblos, like Hawikuh. Many Native peoples refused to give the Spaniards food, and rejected the preaching of the Spanish **friars**. Other peoples tried welcoming the Spaniards in the hopes of avoiding violence.

UP IN THE AIR

+ Acoma Sky City

+ Easy to defend

When the Spaniards reached Acoma Pueblo in what is now New Mexico, they were astonished. The pueblo was built on a mesa, or flat-topped rock, high above the desert floor. The only entrance lay up a narrow staircase carved into the rockface. The Spaniards thought it was the best-protected village they had ever seen. They left the Acoma alone and moved on.

WAR!

☞ **Tiwa resist Spaniards**

☞ **Suffer brutal punishment**

The winter of 1540 was bitterly cold. The freezing Spaniards demanded cloth and blankets from the Tiwa peoples of the Tiguex pueblos. The Tiwa needed the cloth themselves, so they refused. In return, the Spaniards attacked the pueblos. They killed many Tiwa and captured others. They burned their captives alive as a punishment. The Tiwa who could escape fled to the mountains, where they hid until the Spaniards left.

My Explorer Journal

★ **Imagine that you are one of the Pueblo peoples of the Southwest when the Spanish expedition arrives at your village. Would you welcome the strangers and help them, or would you reject their demands for supplies? Give your reasons.**

More Encounters

As the expedition traveled north, Coronado and his men encountered Native peoples who were nomadic. They followed and hunted the buffalo of the Great Plains.

MOVING AROUND

☛ Meeting the Querechos...

☛ ... and the Teyas of Texas

As Coronado crossed the Texas Panhandle in spring 1541, he met the Teyas who lived there. He also met the Teyas' enemies—the nomadic Querechos—who were probably an **Apache** band from Texas (above). These peoples lived by hunting buffalo for their meat and skins. They used the animals' bladders to make water pouches.

AN UNRELIABLE GUIDE

★ Pawnee captive guides Coronado

The Turk, the Pawnee captive who became Coronado's guide, told stories of the magnificent city of Quivira to the northeast. He said it was filled with gold, silver, and fine cloth. When the snows melted, Coronado ordered his men to march to Quivira. It turned out that the Turk's stories were lies. Quivira (in present-day Kansas) was a settlement of grass huts. The furious Spaniards killed the Turk as punishment.

A RICH PEOPLE

+ Home at Quivira

Quivira was home to the Wichita people (below). These farmers did not have the gold and silver Coronado longed for, but they did have rich soil where it was easy to grow crops. The Wichita lived in villages of round houses with grass roofs. They grew corn, beans, and squash, as well as fruits and herbs the Spaniards recognized from Spain. The visitors noted that at the time the Wichita wore very few clothes!

Did you know?

Among the Teyas of Texas was a blind old man who said he had met Spaniards in the past. That suggested that the expedition of Álvar Núñez Cabeza de Vaca in Texas a decade earlier had passed nearby.

SHAGGY COWS

☛ Millions of buffalo roam the plains

As they crossed the Great Plains, the Spaniards saw their first bison, or buffalo. They called the animals "shaggy cows" and noted how Native peoples hunted them (left). The Spaniards came to rely on the buffalo for meat. They also found that piles of buffalo bones made useful markers as they crossed the vast plains.

I Love Nature

The mountains and deserts of New Mexico were familiar to the Spaniards, but they had never seen anything like the Grand Canyon or the Great Plains.

Oops!

When García López de Cárdenas looked down into the Grand Canyon, he guessed that the Colorado River was only 6 ft (1.8 m) wide. In fact, the river is about 300 ft (91 m) wide!

A MIGHTY GORGE

- First Europeans to see Grand Canyon
- Did not make it to canyon floor

In September 1540, Hopi guides led García López de Cárdenas and his men through scrubby forest. Suddenly they reached the South Rim of a vast **gorge**: the Grand Canyon (right). Although the Spaniards tried for three days to reach the canyon floor, they could not find a way down. It was not until 329 years later, in 1869, that the first successful journey along the floor of the Grand Canyon was recorded.

A VAST SEA OF GREEN

★ Great Plains stretch to the horizon

Coronado and his men were also the first Europeans to see the Great Plains. In places, the grass grew taller than the men, and the flat landscape seemed to barely change for hundreds of miles. To the Spanish explorers, the plains all looked the same. They had to use a compass to find their way. However, the Native peoples who lived there had learned to notice features that helped them navigate, such as hollows or changes in the length of the grass.

MONSTERS!

+ Those animals are huge...

+ ... and there are thousands of them!

The Spaniards were astonished not only by the size of the "shaggy cows" they saw on the plains, but also by how many of them there were. One Spaniard called the buffalo "the most monstrous beast ever seen or read about. . . . I do not know what to compare them with unless it be the fish in the sea . . . because the plains were covered with them."

TRAVEL UPDATE

Lost trail

★ If you want to follow the route Coronado took from Hawikuh to Quivira, you are out of luck. Although he followed established Native trails at the start of the journey, the expedition's route across the plains left no trace. The grass grew back over the path. We only know that Coronado reached present-day Lyons, Kansas, before turning around to return to Hawikuh, then to Mexico City in New Spain.

Did you know?

As well as eating many new fruits and vegetables, the Spaniards tried prairie dogs and jackrabbits when their own supply of animals to eat ran out.

WATCH WHAT YOU EAT!

★ **Many plants are familiar**

The Spaniards were amazed by the varied foods of the Native peoples. Coronado's men discovered corn, squash, beans, and turkeys, but sometimes their hunger got the better of them. After eating too many prickly pears (left), they became sick.

Fortune Hunting

Spanish explorers had already found vast riches in Mexico and Peru. Coronado and other young men of his generation also hoped to find wealth for Spain in the New World—and for themselves.

GET RICH QUICK

★ **Coronado marries money...**

★ **... but still wants more**

One of Coronado's main reasons for traveling to the Americas was greed. He became wealthy through his marriage to Beatriz, whose father gave his daughter vast amounts of land. Coronado also wanted to find precious metals, as earlier **conquistadors** had in Mexico and Peru. He used his wife's land as a **guarantee** to raise loans to fund his expedition to find Cibola.

GREEDY, GREEDY

+ **Spanish greed wrecks Native lives**

In Mexico and Peru, the Spanish greed for gold destroyed the Aztec and Inca empires. Native peoples were enslaved by the Europeans as miners or farmers. Many died from exhaustion or from European diseases. In North America, Coronado did not find any gold—but the effects of the Spanish arrival on Native peoples was just as damaging. The Spaniards destroyed settlements and stole their food. They also enslaved many individuals and forced them to act as guides or in other roles. When groups of the Pueblo peoples fled their villages and hid in the mountains until the Spaniards had gone, their ways of life were disrupted. Coronado and his men were desperate to find gold—and they did not care if others suffered as a consequence.

LAND A-PLENTY

- ☛ Coronado finds rich lands...
- ☛ ... but the Spaniards aren't interested

When Coronado realized he was not going to find gold, he started to look for other benefits from his journey. He said of the Tiguex region: "The country is so **fertile** that they do not have to break up the ground the year round, but only have to sow the seed." He called the land at Quivira "the best I have ever seen for producing all the products of Spain." However, the Spanish government was not interested in settling the regions he had explored.

SAVING SOULS

+ Seeking spiritual rewards

Financial profit was not the only reason Spaniards traveled to the New World. Some wanted to gain a spiritual benefit. Spain's rulers aimed to make everyone Catholic. They had already expelled Muslims and Jews from Spain. Now Spanish friars sailed to the New World to spread Christianity. They had limited success. Native peoples had their own beliefs, and few wanted to convert to Catholicism.

My Explorer Journal

★ **Imagine you want to explore the New World. Write to the king of Spain explaining why he should pay for your trip, and describing how your trip might help Spain.**

SPICE ROUTE

★ Coronado hopes to reach India

When Coronado explored the Southwest, silks and spices from Asia were being imported into Europe. These valuable goods were carried from Asia along trade routes that were controlled by Muslims. Like other Spanish explorers in the Americas, Coronado hoped he might find a river that flowed westward that could form a new spice route to Asia. No one yet realized that the vast Pacific Ocean lay between the Americas and Asia!

This Isn't What It Said in the Brochure!

Coronado and his men overcame many difficulties in the harsh conditions of the Southwest. To the government of New Spain, however, the expedition was a failure.

REACHING CIBOLA

- A disappointing arrival
- Violent resistance

When Coronado reached the adobe pueblo of Hawikuh (right) in July 1540, he soon saw it was no city of gold. When he tried to take control of the village, the Zuni fought back. In the fighting, Coronado was seriously hurt when a stone hit his helmet. His troops had to save him from further injury. He never again led his men into action.

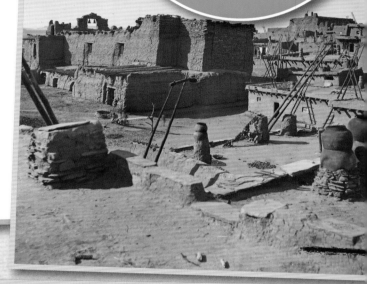

WE'RE HUNGRY

★ Missing the supply ships
★ Spaniards have empty bellies

Coronado planned for his expedition to be resupplied by ship. Alarcón sailed up the Colorado River, as planned, but Coronado's weary men only reached the river two months later—and in the wrong place. There were no food supplies. By the time Coronado left Cibola for Quivira, only 30 of his men and horses were fit enough to make the journey.

WE'RE SO COLD!

+ War over blankets

The winter of 1540 was bitterly cold. Coronado's men did not have enough clothing as they wintered with the Tiwa at Tiguex. Coronado asked for 300 of the blankets the Tiwa wove (right). When the Tiwa did not agree at once, Coronado attacked. The violence ended any chance that the Tiwa would help the Spaniards.

THERE'S NO GOLD

- ☞ **Search for gold gets desperate**
- ☞ **Coronado eager to believe rumors**

When Coronado reached Hawikuh, it was clear that Fray Marcos's stories about the great wealth of Cibola were not true. Coronado refused to accept the truth, however. He was so desperate to find gold that at first he allowed himself to be misled by the Turk. It was only when he saw the grass huts of Quivira months later that Coronado finally had to accept that he had been **gullible**. His own greed had allowed him to be easily convinced by what turned out to be only rumors.

 Weather Forecast

LIFE BELOW ZERO!

One of the lowest points of the expedition came in late 1540. The travelers faced months of snow, blizzards, and freezing temperatures. For men used to a warmer climate, this was a difficult situation. It was made worse by not having adequate clothing or enough food.

End of the Road

Coronado returned to New Spain in 1542, having failed to find treasure. Today, however, his journey through the American Southwest is celebrated as a great feat of exploration.

A SAD HOMECOMING

- ☞ Coronado returns to New Spain broke
- ☞ Disabled by fall from horse

When Coronado returned home, he was virtually broke. He resumed his position as governor of New Galicia, but the tough expedition had left him too sick to do the job well, and so he was fired. He faced an investigation in Mexico City (right) about how he had led his expedition. The Spanish viceroy turned against him, and Coronado was branded a failure. He died in 1554.

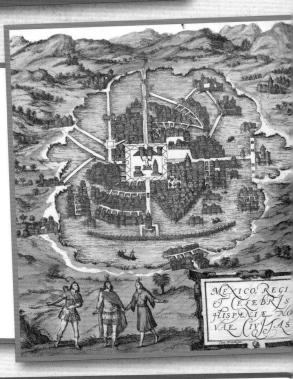

DON'T GO THERE

★ Spaniards turn their attention south

Coronado's failure to find any precious metals stopped Spanish exploration north of New Spain. It would be almost 100 years before explorers headed there. Navajo artists drew these later visitors on rocks (left). Meanwhile, the Spaniards concentrated on their colonies in South America. They **exploited** them until the gold and silver ran out in the 1600s.

YOU'RE NOT WELCOME

+ Native Americans distrust Spaniards

The cruelty shown by Coronado's expedition led to lasting distrust between the different Native peoples and the Spaniards. At Tiguex, for example, the Spaniards attacked the pueblo of Moho in the so-called Tiguex War. García López de Cárdenas burned alive any Tiwa who tried to escape. On his return to Spain in 1545, Cárdenas was sent to jail for excessive cruelty. But the damage had already been done. Peoples like the Tiwa had been badly damaged by their contact with the Spanish. The Spaniards knew they would not be welcome in the Southwest.

My Explorer Journal

★ **Imagine you have returned from traveling with Coronado. Use the evidence in this book to write a letter to the king explaining where you think the mission went wrong, and what could have been done differently.**

A MISSION TO CONVERT

☛ The first parish in America

When Coronado left to return to New Spain, the friar Juan de Padilla (left) stayed behind. He wanted to try to convert local people to Christianity. He became a popular priest among his parishioners. When he tried to leave in November 1544 to convert others, they killed him because they did not want him to leave.

On Trial

After his return to Mexico, Coronado was put on trial for treating Native Americans with excessive cruelty. He was questioned for 40 days. He was fined, but in the end was found not guilty.

GLOSSARY

adobe A kind of clay that is dried and used as a building material

badlands Areas of eroded, rocky land with little vegetation

caravels Small, fast sailing ships

cavalryman A soldiers who fights on horseback

compass A navigation device with a magnetized needle that points to north

conquistadors Spanish adventurers who conquered South America and Mexico

convert To give up one religion for another, or to persuade someone else to do so

empire A large area ruled by the same ruler

enslaved Forced into slavery

estates Areas of land, especially for farming

etiquette The rules of polite behavior and good manners in a particular society

exploited Made full use of something, particularly in an unfair way

fertile Capable of producing many crops

friars Male members of religious orders

gorge A deep, narrow valley with steep walls, and a river or stream at the bottom

guarantee A formal promise that something will happen in the future, such as the payment of a debt

gullible Easily persuaded to believe something

inherited Received money or property from someone after their death

lure To tempt somebody to do something

mesas Isolated, flat-topped hills with straight sides; found in the American Southwest

navigator A person who guides a ship

nomadic Describes people with no permanent home, who instead move from place to place

peninsula A long, thin piece of land projecting into a body of water

plateau A level area of high ground

province An administrative area of a country

pueblo A communal village of interlocking houses with flat roofs; the peoples who live in pueblos are collectively known as the Pueblo

sandbars Underwater sandbanks

turquoise A blue-green semi-precious stone

viceroy Someone who rules an area on behalf of a monarch

Francisco de Coronado is born to a wealthy family in Salamanca, Spain.

Now married and wealthy, Coronado hears stories about Cibola, a "city of gold" to the north.

July: Coronado and his starving men reach Cibola and discover a pueblo village inhabited by the Zuni people.

March: The Tiguex War ends when Coronado attacks the pueblo of Moho. When the Tiwa inhabitants tr to escape, the Spaniards kill them.

1510 **1535** **1539** **1540** **1541**

With few prospects in Spain, Coronado sails to New Spain with the first viceroy, Antonio de Mendoza.

April 22: Coronado leads a large expedition north from Culiacán, the last town at the edge of New Spain

September: A group of Spaniards led by Captain García López de Cárdenas become the first Europeans to see the Grand Canyon.

ON THE WEB

www.history.com/topics/exploration/
francisco-vazquez-de-coronado
History.com page on Coronado with videos
and links.

http://ageofex.marinersmuseum.org/
index.php?type=explorer&id=65
Account of the expedition from the Mariners
Museum.

www.arizonaexperience.org/
remember/coronado-expedition
A summary of Coronado's journey from The
Arizona Experience.

www.nps.gov/coro/planyourvisit/
upload/COROExpeditionmap2.pdf
The National Parks Service downloadable PDF
map of Coronado's journey.

www.mrnussbaum.com/explorers/
coronado/
An interesting biography and video about
Coronado.

BOOKS

Cantor, Carrie Nichols. *Francisco Vásquez de Coronado: The Search for Cities of Gold* (The Hispanic Library). The Child's World, 2003.

Mountjoy, Shane. *Francisco Coronado and the Seven Cities of Gold*. Chelsea House Publishers, 2006.

Petrie, Kristin. *Francisco Vásquez de Coronado* (Explorers). Checkerboard Library, 2004.

Roberts, Steven. *Francisco Vásquez de Coronado* (Junior Graphic Famous Explorers). PowerKids Press, 2013.

August: Coronado leads the expedition across the Plains to find Quivira.

Coronado is disappointed to find that Quivira is a farming village of the Wichita people.

Coronado is put on trial in Mexico City for mistreating Native peoples. His friends on the inquiry help him be found innocent.

1542 **1544** **1554**

Lost on the Great Plains, Coronado sends back most of the expedition and continues to Quivira with a small group.

April: Coronado returns to Mexico City as a failure. The expedition has left him near bankrupt and in poor health.

September 22: Coronado dies of an infectious disease in Mexico City, aged about 44.

INDEX